fluttertongue 3

fluttertongue 3
DISARRAY

by
Steven Ross Smith

TURNSTONE PRESS

Turnstone Press
Artspace Building
607-100 Arthur Street
Winnipeg, MB
R3B 1H3 Canada
www.TurnstonePress.com

Turnstone Press gratefully acknowledges the assistance of The Canada Council for the Arts, the Manitoba Arts Council, the Government of Canada through the Book Publishing Industry Development Program and the Government of Manitoba through the Department of Culture, Heritage and Tourism, Arts Branch, for our publishing activities.

 Canada Council
for the Arts
Conseil des Arts
du Canada

 MANITOBA CONSEIL DES arts COUNCIL DU MANITOBA

Canadä

Cover design: Doowah Design
Interior design: Sharon Caseburg
Printed and bound in Canada by Kromar Printing Ltd. for Turnstone Press.

Library and Archives Canada Cataloguing in Publication

Smith, Steven, 1945-
   Fluttertongue. Book 3: Disarray / Steven Ross Smith.

Poems.
ISBN 0-88801-307-8

   I. Title. II. Title: Disarray.

PS8587.M59F583 2005   C811'.54   C2005-900771-0

To the bold poets who have pushed wider the walls of poetry, enabling me to stretch my own strictures/structures. Many of these poets are visited one way or another in the pieces and notes that follow.

The author would like to thank and acknowledge The Canada Council for the Arts and the Saskatchewan Arts Board, agencies that provided funding, enabling the writer to 'purchase' time required to develop and refine this manuscript. Thanks to Fred Wah for our long conversations and his editorial sensitivity and acuity; to Susan Andrews Grace for her close read, her probing critique, and her affirming comments; and to Karen and Mel for the solitude found at the Ranchita, which enabled the penultimate focus and buffing. Gratitude to my mate, J. Jill Robinson, for many contributions to this work and for pointing me toward some final touches.

To think? . . . To think! It is to lose the thread.

—Paul Valery

May words cease to be arms; means of action, means of salvation.
Let us count, rather, on disarray.

—Maurice Blanchot

fluttertongue 3

syntax stretched out, estranged. but don't break this day's rules. tensions

Grasp. Slide. Drift. Click. Conversation flickers,
infuses, infused with coffee-long chats and mornings,
poetry-long. Syntax stretched out, estranged. Gestures
glancing off the veer of café buzz. Cagean chances in
the vroom of verse where word-glow unreads, undoes
into delirium, uncoils a long frayed rope. Refill, retalk
narrative privilege. Go free. Go improv. Improve on
the already-thought. Froth it with more talk. Pound it.
Marl att. Steam it. Bross ard and spice with the
ubiquitous Ni chol. Nix the cruise control. *Be in the
eddies* Don Mc said. Skitter-scatter prismatic. How to
hold the light long through the word-shift of
a(l)ttitudes. Spinn(oza)ing. Whorl whirl world.
that lurk. resistance offers no answer to reading in and through. time
Journ(al)eying. Bob and weave at the speed of
thought, go dizzy, get the chatter down on coiling
tape. And yang. Lunch late and don't stop listening.

1. For Fred Wah

All around a babble of possibilities,
idiosyncratic, synched to this unfamiliar system. The
poem. Crash. So fresh. A radish breaking on the
tongue. Tang. Eros there. And in the cottonwoods, that
exploding exultation. Seed fluff floating everywhere
like dryer lint. So write. But don't brake. This day's
rules for breaking. Down. Measure with a stick,
Thrower. Stick to it, stay, in the untalkable universe. A
footing. Reader growling—roisterous, roasted. All this
cooked up stuff. Singed. Brute. Bleat. Get singing—let
the throat hear.

for fruit and freedom. when to pluck. communiqués and dogma. cotton

Windstorm. Screen rips apart. Useless language
in the bluster. Ghost-gust free-wheels, chuffs the
waters, churns the bed. Mentalmatter deeper or
shallower. Blast and blow. How far can gust go, can I
go and still thread in? Beep & El's *th'read*, a maze of
A-to-Zed-webbed reading, reading in and through.
Who's organizing standards rule? Links must be more
than stitchery or mirror flips, so I cushion the needle,
cover the glass, try blindness, tie the guiding hand
behind my back as clouds glide, blanket. Nothing
seen in blackout 'til the gust clears the air.
Rustlerattledance. Paperchains, wordchimes sway
and chatter with the breeze. Impossible to read in
batting brain resists even incoherence. other people's words, easy
motion, to jot. Every mote in my view electrifies,
ignites—poplar leaves, needle grasses, purple clover,
sand grains in toes. The river's restlessness, sultry,
lustrous, a-tremble, swollen with desire. Veil-free.
Reverie.

Veer. The verity of house and verse. Sleep passes
unexpectedly through the night, resists waking yet lies
full of anticipation for agents and relatives, a line or
two. Sluggish though. No, not that crawling, slimy,
lover of damp. But slow. A builder, cautious and rash.
Careful and carefree at the same time. Dry. Without a
thought. I (more than one) appears—might not be
me. Are any? Mind appears like teeth in a glass.
Context misleads. Brush scuffling. Longing for that
Shearing fluidity. Such ease in fingers. Sheer soul. Clip,
prune. Time for fruit and freedom, maybe lullabies.
Birds land on the fingers that go numb with age, that
yearn for a paddle, the pull of water. To home. A

answers. circumspect circumlocutionist times. writing destroys certainty.

dream in our hands. Ownership impossible in the end.
Like coherence in chaos, not glue but flux that rules.
Flax that poked through but did not survive the
winter (hard) beside the rue. Fuss, tow, heave.
Concrete time seems the only consistency. Patio,
basement, curb. Write the city about the stagnant
water there, persist. Gears move unhurriedly, but the
Aqueduct bill (culvert) has been paid. Try not to think,
culprit. Or think divert.

Ache there. Bladder wakes the sleeper, pulls him
from a dream through the pressing point. Tiptoe.
Floor squeaks underfoot. Crow talks from the
branches out there. He senses the tenderness, the
wonder of corvid syntax as he gropes into the dark,
tries not to be cautious, to fly with some other
propulsion, to surrender, let go. Cotton batting brain
resists even incoherence. Pressure still there. Leafy
silhouette cast right into the room. Framed dappling
moondance on the floor. *Scree.* Word that slides and
tumbles. Becomes synonymous with Wah in mind,
tries for the line-breaks like a shifting underfoot. Cast
off balance, writes *tippy*. Fred would say *tipsy*'s
right too about the wounding. jagged corners. skin abraded on gravel.
synonym. ---------- Scratched that word out. Why?
What standard? What word? Can't say just anything!
Toxicity? Like maladjusted fruit-fly sperm. Who judges
the *mal*? Chants de, Fleurs de? Add apt words yourself.
Spleen shows in layers. Paris gets to be way back in the
memory net, though this river of ideas seems new.
Drunk with Baudelaire on wine, poetry, *virtue*. "As I
please." Against the weight. Against the blowing down.

7.

I have not looked well enough at your eyelids,
not studied them closely. Nor well enough the poems
of Cendrars and Zukofsky. They knew music. Each
hair must be studied. Each syllable. When I don't look,
don't write, I know what to do. Writing destroys
certainty. Blows the lid off. Writing not knowing. Not
knowing even eyelids. Yours. Or hearing dissonant
chords. Of course it's a question of ear. Of a rhythm
that bobs my head. A flickflack-licketysplit-rail-
clicking ride on the train. Blaise and Louis would
approve. bp too. Cut back for a *trans*-cameo. Can't
remember though forgetting may not exist. Hum
along. Night train. Something will come. James Brown
you are everything that is written, a hostage to yourself. tunnelling down,
will leap up, fling off the cape, and wail *pl-e-e-e-a-a-se
please don't go.* He knows the *vicious circles.* I thought
Blanchot said *the prostitutes of etymology.* Who would
they be? Would their eyelids be lined like Little
Richard's? Like this? A trace of what derivation,
deviation. Listen for the out lines' mumblehum
illusion, the distant track. Eye-stare, tries
splitting hairs with a gazed intent.

15. for bp

Mustard. Sulphur. Honey. Reach to the bush for a lexicon of shades to describe a tree I am sure is turning. *Turning,* I say for shifts in colour. As if motion. Or death, degree of yellow. Name this hue to hold. Needled, ever should be green. Back in my house I'm discoloured. Slipped to the absence of colour, darkened, falling far in shadow. A flailer at apparitions, I dig in. I guess at things. *Larch*? Find out later I'm right. Right too about the wound. Intuition is more than a guess. (Faith, if attended, could root.) Called *tamarack* here—of the family *larix*—going tawny. Instinct tells me this is bog land, and that needles drop. Confused tree hovers between conifer

down. so much of trying to mouth is this way. you are talking here of

and deciduous. I hover too in the depend-upon. One gene, one gesture, one letter can make the difference. Rot. Root. How not to play that needle game, needy game? Not to clamp? What to decide? Drive and drive. A blade through this bush. Fall here, slants me in sunrays with each mile and revelation. Truth a track I stretch on. A glory of rust and green and gold, and behind the glow, melancholy, in shadows. Fall again. Lift. Staunch the wound. Steer out of the dug rut. All water does not swamp and sop. Follow river sheen and ripple. Ripple-light awes. That puncture is deep—is longing, is fury scrubbing in the rapids to rub itself out. Fear wells up rapidissimo. Savour or flee? Aspen

glitters, bejewelled, waves me off. Larch goes bare to
its warty scars. I dash out of the shield. Chill circles
the wheal. Revealed, I tremble. I am bare.

language as if an undreamed-of dream. leaning to fall in the verse

Refusal is the first degree. Becomes your
measure. Resistance. Yet you have learned. Someone
(else) drives you. You shift back, back toward disaster
you anticipate, automatic. You speak of the need for
music and sensory allure, lilt and light flirting,
inflaming the trees, autumn orgasm of russet, gold,
green that shudders the sky, before diminuendo, the
barrening. You speak of compliance, the abandonment
of self. Where *proceeding with a slow and even step,
destroyed men come and go.* How this calls! Scrapes you
in its wearing down. Abrades you back to your eighth
year (a death)—a measure, ostinato which does not
cleave, but opens through all your life, chorusing

groove, into morning, called to its light, lichen-light. silken billow and a

failure. Fall. Familiar rustle underfoot and sweetleaf
muskleaf scent, husky in your nose. Your tongue thick
with seasoning. When limbs are shorn, a stranger
lurks. You shoulder a borrowed coat for disguise,
protection. Though familial you cannot recognize
your self in this guise. A jay shrieks in the ardent red
dogwood. You rage at being someone else. Fury burns
you. You feel the collapse. Refuse again, though your
breath weakens. You are a hostage to yourself taken to
a place of your making that is not your own. Your eye
has closed to all that arouses you. Your ear has turned
from your own lips' incantation. Amidst ardour, this
refusal.

River is absence. Bankless, waterless. Lessing
speaks of brainwashing's advanced techniques that
seep into your hidden crannies when you're not
looking with the third eye (most of the time). Stays
there giving directions. Steers you by tension,
relaxation. Despite bridges. Driving over, you hear the
whisper of emptiness down there. You are in the deep
fog of a memory of river, a dirge of losses. A mournful
song aches in gaps and echoes, the chill of an ice fog
song shaping emptiness as mist makes the lips heavy
with frost, constriction. So much of trying to mouth is
this way. Stiff from the traction of waking and
reawaking. Construction subtle and brutal. The river
glimpse of flow. skin of persimmon. scan the reservoir of words. words,
rigid and in ruins. Fog as you approach is a white
swirl. In its centre all is colourless. Slogans and songs
condense in the cortex. You steer. Press your lips
together. Words in the fog dart blindly, but you keep
speaking them. Fog-washed words.

22.

Seven-part Suite for Robert Kroetsch

Lunar knowledge, I say, *lunar impulse* we share. Near coincidence. Between us, eighteen years less a day. Bone-weary today. Straining out of clerk rut (file this, pay that), leaning to fall in the verse groove. What is the place of the poem in the swell? In the micro-particle careen? Back to that glow, that lunar thing. *First the tide rushes in.* A matter of birth I'm referring to. I count quietly. A number thing. Get that done to hear the poem. To hear the poem *listen for thunder on cloudless days.* In any groove I might sit too low to hear the sounds scudding by. Sitting on a stone in a field, head tilted slightly to favour my good ear, eyes cast down so sight does not mar attention. The moon, inches. crawl from between the covers. day is an empty cup you fall into. visible or not, will inform what's heard—the impossible tone rising.

24.

Raw, beckons. What surrounds, is, is not. Could
just as well not be, or be otherwise. How can you
know, notate, if appearance is disguise? Or absence.
The gaze jumps, settles to wait for words. White trees,
and below lies the river, fixed in your sight, in *the
mathematics of the gaze: angle and tangent,* flowing
away through sloped banks. The bed, though a hidden
lair, is certain, in eye time. River runs from this land,
from your stare. River-skin deludes with ice-crust,
with sheen and opening. A disguise disintegrates to an
earlier disguise you can't remember and mirrors your
amnesia, your arousal. You jot. Silken billowing and a
glimpse of flow. Glance ignites ardour, Eros. You leap
disband the act of hand. all thumbs in song. can wit or attention make
with *a pleased and luminous and violent desire.*
Groundless. Uncladding. Falling to ruin. A dark
skeleton hidden by whiteness. Flash-blind. Wreckage
exposes a new contour. You excavate, dig your blunt
hands in shy rubble. You have never been this close.
Your fingers rake remnants with blind-mole groping.
Ache as you probe the scree. The poem hides beneath
deep longing. Eventually things bare to chewed,
arthritic hands that have become your eyes. They claw
striated air. Your skin though etched with stone-dust,
blood, feels unclad. Its nakedness, clenched, conceals.
*It's a matter of knowing when to look and when not to
look.* Concealment, all there is to reveal.

25. for R.K.

Exactly what happened? I ask your pages. Seek
mirror-struck images for hints of the plot of you. Are
you the poem? The man? Which is which? Which has
been loved by talented women? *You're going to die of*
love, according to Lang, to braggadocio, or to
posturings of the poem-story. The priapic and griping
sad Phoenician, finishing his bawdy tale, body tipsy,
adrift, inchoate (Nichol's road). The page is a window
in the tree house. The poem the lover you bed there.
Words are inches I crawl between the covers. Tips of
myself. This glance, this finger, this nose in words, in
the coupling seen through cracks in the planks.
Snooper for aporrhoea. For truffles or treacherous
feather or bone. gimpy pillows. worthlessness reveals a lack. the long line,
triple entendre. The lovely teachery of words. The
courting chase in the viney field. *The poem must resist*
the poet. Delay learns desire's fervour, waits the small
death. If there is an afterwards, the poem lights up,
turns toward the wall.

27. for R.K.

One, who walks *such edges of the trembling soul.*
The other,　　　*the old*
　　　poet, in his cups
　　　and thinking
Two who are the same poet, on the same day. Twenty-
fifth day of the sixth month. Their day's words draw a
third to hover there. Icon day, from the dayless bone
cradle I squirmed, dazed, into cupped hands, into
calendared worlds. How far had I come when these
words quivered on the threads of that white page
before your eyes? Annum of your entry missing. Day
is an empty cup we fall into, urn for the journey we
carry our ashes forward on, smudging bits of self here
line of longing swallows you toward the unspeakable. the pressured
and there. Dusty stain which, in the day's air, glints.
Mid-step, the *trembling soul* speaks and I turn, glance
over my shoulder. The ones, who preceded, who I
thought I'd left in my dust, are right with me. I walk
between two poem-makers. I gaze, bump shoulders,
think how in youth I tore hell-bent for going. The
jouk, the churning overturning motion that mattered.
Pathbent with no path, but running like the dickens.
Charley horse or no, the body was infallible. Nothing
but *it* mattered. Now I scurry. They walk ahead, at a
pace, though wobbly, breathe easy, scan the view,
listen to crow talk.

"Such nuance!" Eyeing the hovering kingfisher.
"See that strophe?"
he got the color of his breast
from the heat of the setting sun.
Reverence in a glance at one bird, a life as particular as
the old poet's own, as cloistered, as exposed. Nest treed
and shallow, articulate with sticks and string; or
tunnelled to a cup-shaped bed of regurgitated bone.
Particular. We all (mostly) mend from nest amnesia,
birthing (the opening pelvic bone, a space where
silence hovers). Speech becomes possible. From folds,
a bit of scalp, skin, a cry, falls into the white sheet, the
cupping. A feather, a drop. Catch it. *Trembling soul.* I
surround. blazing restlessness. shards. fall to your knees. everything jabs
edge at things, a beggar. A few do not fly from me.
These two who are one. Who bracket me, let me jot. At
my hands, they glance, glance away, tilt back to the
coverts. Ablaze, after many suns, the chest of the canny
bird.

30. for R.K.

Frozen to the plough. Stiff in word furrows. A frown across a forehead's thought. Frosted soil gleams. The blade's knife-edge frets air that whistles between my thumb and fumbling fingers. All thumbs. Green thumb. Sore thumb. Suck it suck it. Friction-it. Fricassee. Fric-fric-fric-fricative. Awk! Word. This buck-back binding stutter. This knuckle-slap's instant regret. Dig. And dig. Despite ear-shattering squeals. Blade at the ice. Meat, metal-caught. Hammering rigid legs free of the machine.

and jabs. everything escapes from frosted windows. in the thicket of

31. for R.K.

The absence, of neglect. Listen at the periphery.
The perilous heights of your enviable wit. Does
witnessing absence negate it? Form presence? I make
light, ha. Wish I had such potency. Or just a pal.
Driving, I am exhausted. So little sleep. So little
reading these days. When I read I read about brome
grass. Grows well in neglect. Green in early spring, late
into fall. I wake early this morning in the verdant light
thinking about mothers. In the death of your mother I
speak to the grass. She could name ducks in the dark
by their talk. *Attention is the natural prayer of the soul.*
Your poems are a prayer to her. Can wit or attention
make feather or bone? The poem whispers from a
noise. *temporary rescue. a steady jagged beat. from you in the form of*
kind of neglect. The sweet wafting lily-of-the-valley
from shade behind the dogwood. *Words are pretenders.*
Men in their solitary spheres cling to women. My
hands are naked on the steering wheel. All this fuel
and speed gets me nowhere. I am in my solitary
sphere, man without man, but for heroes. I pretend. I
garden, a reluctant volunteer, an opportunist who
clings, remora-like, to a word. I, and i pretend *no one is
absent.* Or here. Neglect in my garden produces
prolific Creeping Charley. I yank long and hidden
tendrils certain I'll never find the end. *Niemand,* the
unnameable one, is praised. I hear the shriek and honk
of the wildfowl party on the river, jubilant. It's a
question, as your mother knew, of reverence.

32. for R.K.

Dinner at Marbles. I try not to lose them in the
shuffle of referents. And after pitch and fork at the
circular table scholars and word skullers walk back to
Kroetsch HQ. Place of the story-like gather of tongues.
We are aphoristic, apostolic. Though not apologetic
for our faith. The aporrhoea aurora in full evidence.
We are in session giving tribute, incessant nods to the
tributary with his marvellous acuities, insistences. So
many ideas our minds go almost numb so we stop for
coffee, then start again to peruse the poetics of the
small-hearted writer, rat-a-tat-Rita who writes her way
out of the picture. RK as GS, Gertrude Steins his story
in drag. Dragland loses his text then finds and refuses
postponement and delay. in delay you fence with death, slipping on the
and drags out his ending. Draper a stuttering host,
hostage to Stan's restanding and the uproar of his
wordings. Wordswords honed though no battle is here
but the river. This flow of love, keen as a blade, for the
high plains drafter of those first frisky words on the
frosted fields or cross-dressing a story in which she
(Rita) is absent, disappeared into the coulee, the
treeline. Beeline. Belonging to the long line, line of
longing's song. Buzz of lust busts loose. I would lick
where they work at their nectar, my tongue seeking the
sweetened perfection the word cleaves. The Lang
wedging story. Donnybrook. Hornybook.
Robby'sbook cranes for the whistle from the CNR
bridge, the clickety-clack, the unheard winghum

in Vera's thighs. *Yakety-yak, don't talk back* (Coasters
'58). O that hot sax. O that singing telegram sent by
no one, sent from absence, to find itself in the buzz
when I close my eyes.

slick. without a wish to alter, the shadow of life shows through (release

34. *postscript.* for R.K.

The poem doubles. You must fix it. You try a
hairpin turn, send probes down a throat-road that
mirrors. Same as before but with variations. You
cannot start over once started. Pared lines leave you
less fettered. You plunge from the *bone-ladder* down
air's oesophagus into anguish and terror, into the
chatterbox-pool's water-thin reflection, thick words.
Thoughtless gab bobs you up, bucks you down. You
flop to watch puck-warriors flick sticks and blood in
their blade dance tournaments of nothingness and
ledgers. Childmouths cheer. The circle in a toddler's
hand is a flag-stick, a ball or a seed. That disk at his
feet is a landmine. *The lips of the tombs are alive.* On
us from this trap. recover that gist). disappointment flushes your cheeks.
the spit in the river, migrant white pelicans groom and
raise their huge bills gulping fish. Today sun and
packages arrive. At a knock or ring, trips and tracks
beckon you. A chance to perform. The tongue is a
wagon for words, a puller and prober, syllablelicker,
cheeklumper, fruitrind, stonepit, a carter of skeletons
and rocks, equipment and maps. Throat is a road to
connect. Road is a throat, swallows you toward the
unspeakable. To correct the coordinates, you detour,
bump over sticks and roots and bones. Children are
dying by numbers. Your hands are naked. That scream
far away slices your ears. Is yours. You fall and get up.
Your jammy teeth chatter. You cling to the stone-
wheel, veer, reel, retongue the salt 'til you gag, then
croak a parched articulation. Bleached-bone-speech.

Why am I so full of sorrow? Or full with soberness of being. I have tripped over the bottom line. Overhead, the video machine pumps sephardic shards, eye-slitting slivers. I have bounced up to a lofty view that proffers a certain authority. Nothing is wrong. Everyone is happy and chuckling. Thirty thousand feet won't make me high. I've already sealed the vomit-sac. Or am I unknowingly drugged by plastic rapture? I am above and beneath at the same time. Everyone grounded waits for someone from above. I see the shadow that lurks between dark intrigues and try to plot my way out despite the weight of futility. My senses go dull. There is no ease, *words will not help you. tongues slick through, remove sense. truth is a* no instrument to guide me. No button for up, no switch for the landing gear. Not even a slot for the wordplay that whispers faintly in my ear.

Head aches so, on a rock that pretends to be a
pillow. Word stuck in the lobe that wants to scream
the pain into another aether. Air filled with mist and
rain. Barometer needle spears something you already
know, as everything escapes from you in the form of
a wish. Into the white fumes. You are in the place of
longing and are still longing. You are no match for
yourself. You say you are not who you want to be,
want to be someone you're not. There's been enough
rain. Family is always arriving, departing. A child
learns words at a clip that astounds. But in your skin
the splinter digs deeper. Redness, contusion. You are
swollen, all are swollen with abnegation or plenitude.

fugitive that escapes. everything is about drive and muscle, discord,
Moss flourishes. Slugs slip ecstatic across rocks to
climb and cling on broom-branch-tips in the fecund
world. Blood vessels and tissue around the wound
spasm and swell and the pressure is near unbearable
and none of this gives any rush, any aesthetic release.
Over there, desire paddlestrokes and drips in this
lush land. The forest drools, lips flush with fern and
fringed with fir needles. You slip into the moist kiss
seeking relief from the probe that knows your injury
too well. Cedar-rot cushions your fall.

Salal is prodigious. Green and rubbery.
Almost plastic. The beach is a white blaze, a scythe
blade between green cedar and fir and the sea's steely
blue. Those closest to you are asleep in the cabin on
the small mountain's slope. Yesterday hope left. A
knot to secure slipped off its post. You have limits,
can withstand only so many assaults. Forest curves
around you. Arms or a pillow. Or a huge feathery
bowl. You slide up and down its sides. Fall back and
back. No buffer waits when you are knocked back by
tricks so alien to you. You could depart. Some take to
the sea in all manner of vessels. Low-set and double-
oared, or cocky and jet-fuelled. Or tack a white
dissonance. a variety of chambers. at times terrifying. it's time to
triangle to baffle the wind. She (the journalist) says
that in Algeria families are massacred and daughters
are raped. On your own continent torturers of
children call for understanding and parole. The
duplicity of mercy's caul. You have retreated from
the horror. And from your undeserved strife. You
feel protected by your silence. By still trees. On thin
beach blade, shells of lives lie crushed, so white,
licked and dashed by restless wave-tongues, beauty
by caress and turbulence. Broken by the sea's kiss. In
the contradiction, you reach for a place that is your
own, extend your hand without a wish to alter or
manipulate. Where who you are reaches clearly into
someone's world. The forest at the sea's back is your

desire, verdant, speaking itself in wind-shimmer,
giving itself, promiscuous, to any lover. Vibrant and
naïve, intention-free.

unbutton. fingertip caress is novelty. the wearing familiar. you wear this

Last night. The poetry was okay but there was
too much chatter; poems yoked in exegesis; the joke
about eggs made before. Out of this, so little light.
How to shift that slight bit to true sight. To see: bird
as messenger; spear of glint in my lover's eye; sheen of
her skin. Some egg shells are so thin, when held to
light, the shadow of life shows through. I am without
good music, though can imagine it, almost. A dog's
feet pad-click across the wood floor. I hear toenails.
John Cage would hear music. Mail takes a bite out of
my desk where forgetting's teeth sink in. Perhaps
intention can never be undermined. Syntactic
intention logs. Where is the jam, the juxta-collision?
thinning self, shrinking. or the word anguish. no sense of fashion. you
Children move me beyond the person I thought I
was, yet this reads like a list. Is there anything random
in the programmed brain? My mouth dries. I croak as
I begin to speak. Who is the first person referent?
What joke? she asks. (The one about divine seeds,
Jesus' eggs—get it?) *Go on. Get away. Get out.* Words
almost the same can mean different things, given
intonation and context. In that case, where do I set the
poem? In a few minutes the proof-work begins. I will
shift with the display-cracks that un-nerve me.

42. for bp

You arrive and depart at the same time. Carried
on bus-rumble and language, carried past cows, bales,
and the fireball-sun that wows the horizon. Things
you can name hover. Last evening was about absence.
Where your words hung, in the room of empty chairs.
Friends and acquaintances lost to your ken. The frozen
surface of the pond glares. Faces smile from the void.
Shapes lie in the median—road kill, feigning sleep.
You mourn. You are an author. (You are the written.)
The land is flat, load-bearing. Mountains crouch out
of sight distanced to the west. Everything crouches
behind you. Even the promise of response. But the
screen draws your eye. Jolt and primary colours. (The
can hammer, snap yashica, pummel the shrubbery, can wish. things
unframed world in shades of grey and waxed paper.)
You have been lured. Disappointment burns your
cheeks. Roads cross and leave you shredded.
Everything is scenery with holes. You hear music,
music sings though distant to your ear. You jot, toil
toward witness of dancing fugitive tones that whisper
with incomprehensible buzz, like lips against wax
paper folded on a comb. Many words tingle with the
colour blue. You try to fill their shades with your
attention. So tough when empty chairs have eyes that
stare. You speak to few. Their eyes are your eyes. They
squint toward your speech. Your inaudible collapse.

You give up things. Or they are taken, the
unexpected result. You pretend this is not so. You turn
to the old way. The twist is torture. You prefer this to
letting go. The only you you know is torn away. Shred
from you, adornments fly off. Your arms are a flurry of
grasping. But a weight sits on your head. You are
angry, short-tempered, unkind to those you love. This
is the new you. You do not recognize him but you like
his ugly company. The stock market tumbles. Mercury
drops in the thermometer to thirty below. Night
means nothing to day but definition. You are on the
other side of something else. You will get up, turn
around and still be there. Words will not help you.

disappear. if a miracle occurs, ghosted in the shadowy corner, furtive and

Improvisation will not help you. Loss impoverishes
you. Denial makes you poorer. Nothing improves in
this poverty. There is no you in the empty pocket. In
the leadenness. All you have been is without substance
now. Loss is the footstone. In your blindness you have
stumbled. There is lightness to find by not lifting,
space to step into without bending a knee, a word to
be uttered by the still tongue. You must see this.
Everything is rust. Everything vanishes as dusk turns
to nightfall. You stand, glance back, your shadow is
already gone.

47.

This is the hour of hallucinations. Lights that
split from you seem to rocket through a field or take
to the sky and blink off, gone from your blasted gaze.
You are dim to yourself in this twilight. Nothing to
recognize. You are gone from what you know. From
everyone. Who might you be? You assume that
direction is inevitable, but you bump and everything
falls. The note roars on and rubber hums. Sounds
tread and separate. Alien aircraft stalk. Oil rigs gleam
behind hunky cows, heads down in the frosted grass.
Everything is about drive and muscle. You'd rather
sleep. And beyond the field, two deer stand, twitch-
eared silhouettes on a ridge. They might fly, already
rubbing her pale hands. keep your eye on. rain is a symphony of surfaces
close to the sky.

I was thinking of you in the Garden Flat in
Moffatt, in Scotland. That a poem might be there. Out
your window. Or in your wee den on your drawing
table. Seems so distant. I was reaching for music, back
to Toronto, '78, Jerome Rothenberg soaping up the
silence, inviting me into the lilt of the *Navajo Horse-
Songs of Frank Mitchell.* I long to hear them. Again.
Before the tones fade from my inner ear. I think the
Scots would understand them. I will write into the
void to locate. You, across the immense blue cosmos of
ocean, could be making dinner now, listening to
Scarlatti, as your sun sets and my sun breaks through
the window and the silhouette of Gertrude Stein
slipping through the sieve of time. melody sliced in sections. other voices
hovers here, peering in. I think she has an
appointment with Mitchell. He'll pay his respects.
She's likely to unbutton her cleverness. Tenderly. Show
her tansies. Meanwhile you gaze on winter pansies
outside your door, and "blue tits and chaffinches at
the feeder," as you say in your letter. Distance and
connection, when you dwell on them, are ungraspable,
though the mind travels. Mine breaks out into words.
Your window breaks onto the River Annan. And when
you walk, sometimes you go along the road and
through boggy heather up Hart Fell, to chafing wind
and blue sky. Heart full. The height reached. Heart fall.
I have tumbled into my own house, searching for my
heart. Sometimes I find it and am surprised. From

here I can almost see your view. Can watch your brush
strokes. Do you have lilacs? Madame Gertrude asks
after this. A question of abundance. And your window.

panting, praying. a bullet in the wrist, the gripping fist, the sneer, the

50. for Catherine Macaulay

You have been many people, according to
pictures. Sun is a gold band beneath clouds. You feel
as if you could compose forever in this way. You on
the trike, maybe four, with composure. You and your
first gal at twelve. You and G.T., the soon-to-be-gone
buddy, dapper in ties, thirteen with slick hair and
shiny shoes. You magnify and look for yourself in the
crowd. What touches you you have searched for.
Seared for. The passing of that first love is sorrow. O!
Ch-ch-ch. You and G.T., train-hopping, an acute
thrill recall, an ache in you. O to dwell in that
innocence. Now wheels pull in all directions. The
band widens. Glint is not always gold. All you see is
knife, the jump-bombs. dark corners and clanging. seared, repentant,
resonant and in the vibration nothing stands still
enough for a picture. What falls to the film falls away.
Filmed over. Flimflam sleight of light's shift. You
ache for those people you were. And those who
surround at your party. You were four, twelve, thirteen,
always with friends. You loved—that tricycle
(outgrown), her (sent away), him (fallen)—then and
after. You have loved many things and people since.
Such a crowd. Gold spills into your room, precious,
belonging to everyone who slips away. They tug at
you. You dress up. The occasion is always new though
you tire of novelty, the wearing familiar. You wear
thinning filament. You sit and ready yourself to repeat
the predictable. You want not to go, but to know

where you're going. You never wanted to leave those
moments behind. They left you in a thievery you gave
yourself to without wit, without choice. Such it is. You
stock the cupboard. You hoard. But wealth goes
and goes.

sucked down. tortured vocal chords. do the flowers talk, blow away

To what does the poem attest? In and in. She says *let me in that house.* I say *it is not a house and there is no way in.* It is outside all of us. It is attendance. Mute and empty of intention. You can hammer. Can wish. You can flutter. The poem intones, invents a listener's possibility. *I am not there,* she says. *Where are you?* I ask. *I am absent.* The poem is absence, is that rare summer bird overwintering you've heard but not seen. Common yellowthroat perhaps. Or oriole. You can only guess. Eating ash berries, skin peeled, turned inside out. This membrane is not a house. Is not even membrane. Is what's escaped in the flaying, in the flaughtering light at the edge of your eye. I spring to *your troubles. under tongue vibration waits. a bubble that history moves* words. The familiar. Family even. Seek a mooring in the names of figures I recognize—woman, baby, father. Names that are part of my name. I have been fooled. Try to shift back. Back and back. Be nameless in this skin, be wordless, a beggar before the thrum. My lungs gasp, driven by blood, thirsty for oxygen. (This is life but not biography.) Air is too cold for the late migrant, and food is scarce. The bird dies quietly, invisibly, his feather-light husk tumbling down and down in the bramble, to nestle in the crux. Not one of us is there. The poem escapes again in a whisper. Is less than her name that breathes through my lips. I hold while I lean toward surrender, let go of walls, of spoons, the gleam of her eyes. I am here but not here. Alongside, I attend the disappearance.

52. for Jill

The idea gone. Eaten down at breakfast. With
porridge, eggs, and toast. Something about the
maze. Being here. Abbeying. Adjoining lives. Monks,
writers, painters. Ordered gestures. The maze is out
there, along the road, the narrow path among
conifers. You probe and widening takes place. In
silence you scribble and lines find their own sound.
The shade of morning is grey, brightened by
snowflakes dancing. You force. Not the snow but the
scribble. You reduce effort. You play solitaire. Last
night you dreamt of a distant friend. He'd changed,
grown a dark beard. He was sharp and on-the-go,
still with a camera to his eye, and leaning to the
inside. a bending and a pulling place, spatter and gaffe hooking in.
telephone. In the café you and he talked, sipping
coffee. In the intervals, you watch. In a shadowy
corner a woman, ghostly and furtive, rubbed her
pale hands. Who was she? Perhaps a sign. First dream
in a week of restlessness. You shuffle cards. One week
with self and words, and the bruise heals. One more
week and you might be clear. But home calls. You
would plunge deeper into the maze daily and
somehow come out of yourself. But you choose to
go home to love's emergency, despite the need for
recovery, uncovery. You will return to the world's
weight. Watch ecstasy dance through the rear window,
away. The cards will refuse to align. News will slip in,
will distance you from Fra Angelico's *Annunciation*.
From the angel's poised hands. From her moment

when news was of the spirit, a struggling ground.
Today, out there, all is flash and posture, gossip and
death. You are here. Porridge sweet and sticky. You step
to the shower to wash it from your lips. Begin to hum.
In the café jukebox in your head John Prine drones
back and forth singing his lawless smile. You grin. The
dream washes away. Bruises wash away. Your hair wet,
your face turns up to the spray that disguises tears. In
drizzle you hear spirits, mystics whispering. You gather
yourself as the bells ring. You reach for a towel. Monks
kneel in the chapel. They cross themselves, rise up,
break into song.

stealth jets over Innu. in cindering eyes. cough. carry on. cluttered with

I am wet by the rain in Blodgett's *aria*. The page
curls to the shape of drenched air, the words seep in
through my fingertips. Blossoms stand beneath
inscribing birds. Piano keys, nearby, hold still, in this
season of silence. Passage brings us to stillness. Silence
settles though the air throbs with what lies beneath
sound. I listen. I hear only myself, my small tones. I
turn my ear outward to rain, a symphony of surfaces.
Cedar rail, lilac leaf, loamy earth. I hear this. Through
it try to hear other distance. Rain is tears in this song.
Rain is a memory note to my nine-year-old self.
Sundays, grey days that closed in on me, sent me
gasping toward light and an open door, and at twenty-

assumption. strain for the sur-music, tongue-strung between the slats

five, wheezing for air, and now there seems so much
rain though the wilderness shrinks. And those who've
passed have entered that wild place that terrifies us, we
who are left behind. Wild order we do not understand,
though it stokes our ardour. I have strayed from
listening. Again. Rain is the screen through which an
opening may be gained, a note distilled. Such
discipline demands the patience of guardian trees
though the guerdons are small enough to be missed
and lost forever. I attend and in attention I grow
wetter. Eye and ear a trough. I become near wet as
rain. My hand a cup to cover. A cup to catch.

55. for E.D. Blodgett

I would hurry to this. Scurry
to the crank and twist. Churn
it out. Such falsity. I must   wait.
With the patience of glaciers.
With the confidence of a mountain
Wait.   Wait
Not in anticipation
But in completeness.
No waiting can be
measured.   In the absence of
the gripping fist, the urging shoulder is
stillness.
Ice-still.   Rock-still.   And in time
and bars that speak of confinement. new vectors fracture a song.
the ice-trail   discloses. I long to be beyond
patience.
How to still?   How to hear without listening?
The glacier whispers
                              its way.
The mountain speaks.
                              What tongue?
How to reach without reaching.   To be beyond
longing.
In the mouth of desire
                              And empty of need

K, I
hear you again after all this
time, sixteen trips around the sun. In lines of
Nichol that reach for Chicago, for Ornette
Coleman, for the dark corners and clang of
(your) Kagel songs. Metal was in the
room that night.
Squeals stretched lips against teeth. Raw
of language in the shat-
ter of *k-k-k-k,* the *g-g-g* gurgle-throat,
the gulp of *ol-ol*
Age separates us. Exhaustion nods in what appears to
be communion.

utterance is loss. words fall apart in the mouth, memory forgets. fear is

I would o-d on your songs if I could find more.
H-huh-h escapes my chest. Sounds sandpaper throats.
Mayakovsky's hammer in the palm splinters
woodgrain. Dog-whimper. Budding tree-hum. Scat-
song skitting toward escape. Descending soprano
slide. Slag-ride on the *wwwwaiaiaiaiaillllllllliinng.*
Kag and Nick, your calls and crashes siren-in,
sizzle us, stretch us from
beyond. To be
awed.

58. for Mauricio Kagel, & You too Nicky

I-deology wrestles with cases. Packing crates,
steamer trunks. The burden of self and designation,
dexterous. I deal from left or right, upper or lower.
Birth here, a kind of eye-I-ball of emerging form.
Which i/I tumbles out? Which am i/I? I type i, revise
to I, eye, all along, preferring i. The poem writes me. I
am not the first to say this. 'Me' easier than 'i'. Do I
mean it? And what do I mean? Poem the I and I the
blind search. Bind. Double bind. Caught up in I-
dentity. If the poem writes me does it invent me,
invert me? Like Dylan's tortured vocal chords, his
worn baggage-songs inventing him in my ear that
unhears the message. On the carousel, medium moves
all that's touched. the cast-off home recoils, frails in the friction. you are
to foreground. Ear leads beyond I to eye and sightless
second sight. Or avoidance. Dance the I avows, dance
the ego-sack jives around its I. All invention and
deception. Poem is a song that supplants me. I,
another. A hum, an evocation that d(e)rives (me) out
of my mind-box. A collection of phonemes that bribes
a phony me. Fa-la-la. Decked (to ship) out. The dealer
(I) eyes me.

Leaf, brittle, thinned, trembles on a lilac branch.
Nearby, a swaying spruce hisses, ecstatic. River
articulates the descent of geese, their raucous honks,
an ancient glossolalia. Whisper of a mist of rain.
Amidst this, I strain toward a song that eludes my
song. Mouth longs toward it, feels only the moment's
breath. As my lips quiver, the whorls of my thin ear's
precinct strain for the sur-music. Spruce stills as if to
aid me. Geese settle. Sky gathers its grey veil. I crane
my senses, web-eyed, leaf-eared. Body-song wells.
Tongue bears a thorn.

wound, a glide of edges, bloom, and decay's erasure. desire's spiral. your

60.

White-throated sparrow is a gate-hinge song
that swings to me from a niche in the dehiscent
green. A concealed whistler tunes my ear to melody
and draws my binoculars to scan for the
megaphone-beak, the throat that croons. But the
tunester is not to be seen. I flip to the page in
Stokes' guide book that describes the songsound as
sweet sweet Canada Canada Canada, a rendering
of rhythm into words. Staccato air I hover in, full
of pulses of flutter-wings and warbles, in the
throat-sprung vector where definition is direction,
not destination. Now a flock, a cluster of white-
collared crooners, a choir in my yard, a flap of
mind tastes skin. new skin beyond adjectives. nuance. skin with
feathery robes in the verdant dome. But I still
forage for my own voice. Peck at usable strategies
to get to song, to get beyond the limitation of words.
I grope toward a zone where my throat outreaches
my brain, toward tones that flutter in whiteness that
lingers between the slats and bars that speak of
confinement. I swing, erratic, somewhere beyond
myself, almost out there, where the hidden throat
throbs.

I am at the end. Identity is a question spliced within syllables and sliced away. Hero words have carved and exhausted themselves, are clustered tailings exposed, raw, in the sterile field. No parasites hover. It is fall, on the frost-turned-up collar of winter. Each dark wordbody wants to be still, invisible, wants to be itself and out of service. In this departure, parts of *I* go elemental, ordered by air or earth or water. Costumes slip off the shoulder and hip. *I* is threatened with nakedness, with loss. *I* clutches at any cover but fear is all that's touched and the hour is late. What began at the wordstream has come between *I* and the solid bank. I can hear it sluicing beyond the trees, beyond strangeness at your tongue's touch. light-headed allure. whisper of the magpie's nasal gab. That water, chilled over stone, mutters in crisp air, slices the stiff land, calls *I* to its frigid undertow, to tumble—wordless, a castaway, rigid, bereft.

Diptych. For bpNichol

I unstring words in furrows, go unretentive in
chancy currents. Give in to careen. I conjure
movement in a room, fumble at contemplation,
composing. I Polaroid you into the picture, standing,
yes, here by the French doors, by my telephone table,
on the moss-green carpet. You smile, don't speak. I
look down at my lines then back to your lips. *What the
eye seizes as real is fractured again and again.*
Soundless, your lips shape the words *"Give in."* I nod,
through an ache, an anxiety that splinters. *"Out of
fracture."* Or did I imagine?   Then, no more words,
maybe a rasping *h* overhead, a hum to my left. Is it
wind? Machine? I tilt from the sound, open your
eagle shadow. orange orchids. riff. tongue. aching to break. lovers drift,
book—*Craft Dinner*—(for hunger), open to a scene:
you on the road encountering the figure who says *you
should be writing things down.* I spring to it, write as
fast as I can but SNAP goes the recoil. I am wound. You
didn't like my poems, the *blind* ones, their abstraction.
Perhaps absorption has led me to *the frontiers of
madness.* I squint—(I've been squinting for days). You
are gone. Music whispers from the spot you stood
(you were rarely that quiet). A latch rattles, *the
farmhouse door bangs against the skull.* I steady myself.
Move to prop the door. Let whatever wants in, in; out,
out.

65.

Ear is a tiny canal, open for grand design,
jammed in the multichannel universe. I shape by ear
in bursts of thought, punt borrowed notes, burrow
inside-out to cleanse the cluttered whorl with what it
hears within. Or at edges. A few marks scratch out a
score, and spaces between—signs for swell and
diminishment, bloom and decay. Erasure. Hand rubs
and rubs, scrapes. The pencil is deaf, the hand a
deformed ear.

their own filaments floating, substanceless in your attention. falling

67. for bpN

You're on the kilometric line too long. Long
out of the gate. Out here you huckster words.
Beyond Dogen's wisdom or Stevens' ways, all
thirteen. Or centuries. The backbeat of *poésie*. You
pause there then skip again to the pulse. Blackbird's
wingbeats. Sky leans on you. Your shoulder aches in
the cool grey. You shrug to shun creeping adjectives,
but you are full of them. You do not long for home,
but for its routine. The end of a stanza, a suite
haunts as you amble in Alberta, delivering an iamb
here or there and some spontaneous bleats. Your
café metaphors are male. *Time to kill.* Coffee with *a*
punch. And you don't even mean it. Or do you? You
behind your own beliefs. sensation sifts through something else.
try to impress as you imagine your waiter's black
underthings, blonde hair let down to her shoulders.
Lonely clichés burrow into you, and you have the
nerve or its lack to write them down. And what of
transcendence?   Bridge work crosses Lethe's
leathery strip that snakes grasses and woods. Rain
drenches the land-skin with its lotion. Word-notions
spread everywhere. Skin of sense scales the ironwork,
yet ink chips away. Mountains, white and distant blue,
dance to whispered music you cannot hear. Peaks
beckon with further metaphor as your scratchings
jitter to the bumpy blacktop underneath. In the
foreground of your eyes' range, lovers touch and kiss.
You are no lover but long to be. You, alone, with
desire rising. Or is it pain you'd salve with her

amber-eyed charm and thick accent that utters
the exotic you can practically taste? Skin new skin
skin beyond adjectives skin with strangeness at your
tongue's touch. Skim and probe. Yes. This is what you
want from mountains. To rise on strange skin, and
on your lips a new taste in heady air. Tang of a poem-
probe with all the right words. But you're accentless,
speechless, dumb before mountains and desire.
Or is it hunger?   You are drowsy. Weak and
impoverished. Driven. No one to blame. Not the
weather. The jagged height. Her pinned-up hair.
The backbeat. Not the sky. Nothing to blame (but
yourself). Not even your constant displacement.
you create remains. cross the bone-trestle. salt formations grow.

You wait, a face in the window. Your gaze drifts
to distant evergreens, then back to your reflected face
looking deep into distances. You are a long way from
those you know most well. You are among tall trees,
sweet cedar musk, the prolific webs of spiders
spinning sunlight. You are among birds that keep their
distance, but sing to you. You are waiting, wondering
what to do next. The spider is an acrobat, an
opportunist. He is brown and yellow and works
outward from a small ball of silk in the centre of his
design. He may be she. You know too little. Her genius
and the breeze and unimaginable strength build a
miracle in air. The spider is a ritualist. It can take
torsion (distortion) that drives. you are unravelling over the boulder
hours. You wait, watching. Words drift, their own
filaments floating, elusive despite your attention. You
have been here before, but never at peace. Light dances
in tall tawny grasses, flutters in cedar and spruce. You
wait because wise ones have said that this is the way.
You question. The web shimmers. The pressure of
your place in the human world itches to draw you to
its angst. You stand still, imitate the tree. You are a
poor actor. So lightly rooted, so arm-weary. As the
light shifts, your face disappears from the pane. The
spider pays no heed.

I fly, almost, my toes threaded to a height of
land. It is spring. I am a futurist. Everything is action.
Anything is possible. I live in flux, *and I shall be
renewed by salt* and machines. And their separateness,
my halves. Amoeba to zoetrope. The fissure, H-shaped
(in the brain), its thin bridge crossed by impulses,
lizards. Syllables want to play in the rime, find
connection, buds, a tongue to keep them going, keep
them leaping the span of breath into my morning.
Lizard brain. Desert tongue. Lizard on the salt flats.
Reptilian cortex in a poet's skull. On the other side, if
discovered I shall be baked, pickled, finis. Blunt end
(just ahead), hence resistance, my churn. Yet

field. hell-bent. (no violence.) sage greening in soil. purple violets.

everything sheds. I cross the bone-trestle, twist to
hold myself upright to flee the clock-face corrosion.
Scales shingle, ahead and behind me with each
second-hand skip. Stains, madness. I'm up (to no
good). Below, at my toes, soil drops off. Lizard, a
tongue-flicker. I lose track of my field because
emptiness swallows the standing-ground. I'm shallow-
rooted, dry. I create remains. *I'll taste the* (salt-lick)
dreams as they dissolve, *blown with the dust.*

Jewel-feathered air bristles the dark brigade of
sentinel spruce beyond snow-dusted tawny lawns. First
hoar frost. Closer, the ecstatic locust tree shows off. This
at the end of a rasping night, blackness filled with hoarse
persistent cough. This at the end of any wish for speech.
This at the absence of desire. You barely exist. What
remains moves toward the exit. A drastic possibility. You
wish for a sign in your weariness, a quiver. Out there a
branch shivers. Or is it a trick of eye? You wait. Stillness
overcomes. You are static but unravelling. You are nearby
what matters. Close, but. Books come unbound. The
huge lexicon leaps from the shelf, thuds to the floor.
This motivates you. You bend to its splay, check for
shrapnel. purpling skin. weightless ceiling of the dark grasps you as you
damage, finger its irresistible words arousing your
lust for syllables. They doctor you. They become your
dendritic reach, your crystalline formations. Voices
outside draw you to your window. Strangers pass by on
the shovelled sidewalk beside the lawn. The bells'
exuberant chimes, their peals of joy call everyone to the
occasion, call you to present yourself. No one looks to
your window in their longing for a threshold. They pass,
enter the arched doors, certain of song and the body of
Christ on their tongues. You know this though you are
extrinsic. You will stay aside. Stay flat and blank. Never
mind their (your) ailments. Your irritated throat is a
threat to the white exultation. You blink. A fog is
creeping in. You will be safe in its curtain if you cover
your mouth.

How still the wing leaning bodiless into the
wheal. The break. You are a blue lad who falls, tripped
by her repose. Your feet leave earth. How still her
resting hand. Her delicate fingers barely touch your
name. Her gaze glances off you and away. Her prickly
reserve entices you, pales you, flakes you to multiples.
You crack, an earthless, sealess dry shell, a brittle
scapular. As you fall, the dried-putty coolness of her
hand grasps you. This holding, haunting goddess. You,
the addled coral ladder crumbling, try to pull yourself
together. Thread and feather, pebble and bone all
scatter in this aether. You grasp, strain for re-
attachment, call to her, that she might help you glide
fall, awe-struck, negotiating. hammer age. just-too-late glimpse. you
in the ply of her careless eyes. That she might see
beneath the crust that deadens the wing. Its stiff
utility.

73. Still Life

Deepening awareness sends you to bed spurred
by knowledge of effects of exhaustion. You give up
control, stop avoiding sleep. It is not enough as the
voices are still speaking. This week, Nichol, Celan, and
Halfe. They inhabit, speak into the dark you fear, into
your dreams. You feel near ending, a waiting . . . *if you
wait out the dream the waking comes.* Some motion
pushes, despite your withdrawal. "Rhythm" Daphne
said. Beat that propels, goes strong even when the
words have failed. Footsteps scurry in your house.
Other tasks could compel, reward with tangible work
and result. A sandstorm of sparrows blizzards the
deck. One bird monopolizes the feeder. It could be you
struggle against disarray. not the world way if there's no fix. imagine
taking up all the room. Yes it is you, elbowing out the
poems. How will you end, then begin again, while
scratching repeatedly at the same thing. A dog at his
wound. The deep ache and weight of your half century
of mismanagement. Your anguish. Your guilt. Oh how
you whine. Sparrows fight at the feeder, one bird
trying to own a thousand seeds. Greed or survival
drives him to posture and be fierce with his kind. In
the frenzy seeds spray and other birds are fed. Your
desk is a mess—hardly room to write—mind is a
mess, cluttered and weary (though you claim to have
slept). You struggle against disarray, imagine that
order will come in just a few weeks fulfilling your wish
to leave the room neat behind you, but you are tired,

frightened of sickness. *Of the last wings.* The festive season is ahead, with its dream of *comfort and joy,* though your brain closes down at the dim thought of another obligation, too depleted for desperation. The birds will return later this afternoon, and again tomorrow. Many will come as long as there is food. Too many for you to notice the ones who are gone. Voices still speak to you. *Night has no shadow.* You put out seed.

that order will come in just a few weeks, locked to your intention.

Alike, she and I, in our nakedness pressed to
the red wall, panting, praying to the gods of our
skins' sizzle and gleam. An early key turns in the
door, and our slam of red-faced excuse. A man shifts
and slips through the centre of the oval, his face
turns a colourless question. A scape that sketches me.
Ashen and a sting of red. And blues in the night.
Bobby Blue Bland bawls, belts out his smoothgravel
voice. A car bullets down the straightaway, firing its
twin lucky numbers into my young eyes. Our eyes,
hers and mine. Gentile-eyes, Jewish-eyes. Cool
slivers slide to my lips. Cross the line to the blaze-
glow. Deep as pitch. Despite disapproval (of
bold link. sweetmeat of a lobe. o-d. is grapefruit-bright and fast.
difference). Echo of nightblue. Forbidden fire. We
fumble away in combustion-dust; he drives in
circles, a smoke-curl, racing the small oval in his
souped-up stock, aiming to carry the flag on the
victory lap before heading to the pit. I get blue. I
turn to her large doleful eyes in a crowd. Ice-buffed
light falls into the red-walled room. In my parents'
house. In memory, yellowbright. A chamber song,
that blue stretch. The car is grapefruit-bright and
fast. I'm at the asphalt's edge with the uncle who
holds my hand. My hero Norm Brioux turns left and
left, right hand and leg gearing up and down around
the track. My room this night visited by lust, its red
wall, smouldering red, at the head of the bed. Roiling

volcanic fire. Round and round and yellow. His voice cool as shearing ice. Stoked to it. His chant a glacial lozenge. The car crackles and pops shifting into the danger of the banked turn. The room pulses, our red burning skins (alike) in the dark. Everything turns again and again. Was it Bobby sang that? We crossed the threshold, she and I. Wide as the ribbon drift of a held note.

you were at track's edge. thud in your chest. scurry. the word is the

Grow more heavy. Be more light. Boulder-
weighted. Freight makes itself evident opposing me.
Or is it me at myself? My own tonnage. Rocks
everywhere. Stones in my mouth block syllables.
Tongue-sputter jumbles over the chunk, unable to say
the word it knew, tongue disguised from itself. It wore
a hat, was mistaken. Or was it my wife (the woman I
love) on my head? (Never mind the jokes.) I don't
have one for the season. It's getting harder now as
intention creeps in. (With flaps.) I am stone-burdened
with all I have done before. And my inability. I am
muted, mated to words that weigh or melt away. I
rummage in books for some new ones to build on, to
first dilemma, coughed in chilled air. gripping fist. nape of his neck. te
unblock, make me looser, word-wise, volcanic. Stone-
molten. She says I gush about writing. I say I am *in the
moment's* flow. The word is the first burst, the first
dilemma. I concoct scrim and foreground, stonegrind
the syllables into my own concatenated utterance,
even if I can't pronounce the result. Even if it's a
transient clot in my circuitry. Even if I've depleted the
supply. Perhaps it's time for restraint, to trim and buff.
Like New Year's resolutions to cut back. Yes! The year
will be lean. Pared. With refined technique. On with
the lava-lamp-giddy weightlessness. I'll be lilt-
tongued, nimble with familiarity. I'll dance on the
clotted lava-cap that waits to blow me into light.

79.

Your voice is air and water. All this and nothing
in the speaking you have become, striving to speak
past your old self. Have you become self or someone
else? Or no one. If you find your voice close to speech,
breathe it or slide it over your tongue past the lips. It
becomes our voice, we become lovers, but you are
gone. Tell me who hovers there, in that space, whose
mouthing speaks to me as myself speaking to you.
Forget tricks and wit. You are gone, without. Empty
and emptier. Limited, so (perhaps) limitless. You
must locate in a new mouth that is your old mouth
and begin with a single gasp and in that gasp discern a
voice that is true, and adding syllables, *tiny eternities,*
deum. down of thistle. syllable scoured for. other people's words.
one by one, come to utterance, the trance in words,
drawn, hove to air   hovering.

80.

over the river   that osprey

    ray-
       caught

               hovers

wingquiver   wetspray   prayer   loom-in-air

   allure   illumined   O

our eyes, alight   airlight   lift

         air-
untethered, close to speech, breathing or sliding over your tongue,
         roused

            e-
           ros
              e-
               lysium

81. for Tim Lilburn

*Show Business: Show up, look good, take care of
business!* says Ruth Brown, black and bluesful diva, all
biz and show. She could wail. Give your moneysworth,
your measure of coin, or bloodstream detonation that
jolts your head-bob, leg-twitch, palm-slap and clap.
Beat that ignites a buzz. She understood the biz. Ruth
knew how to work a mike and a room. Across town
Long John Cage pulsed, writing with or without
syntax. He once miked a cactus and invited a
drummer to tweak the spikes. It was music,
cactophany. He put screws and pads in piano strings
and said *it's prepared, play on.* He threw coins and
wrote the patterns as melody. He sang the psalms of
heard from the moment's prisonhouse, a rankle in conditions. your
the future. Spasm songs that broke, detoning,
retoning, on the new ear, returning us to
unpredictables. I think Ruth Brown is his heroine.
Henri Chopin must know her too. With Parisian
panache he swallowed a microphone to hear his
interior songs. Made recordings, throbbing odes,
gutsy pronouncements. He is a small man, but says,
la poésie, c'est moi. Il donne le spectacle. Vous savez
ce qu'il a compris—Ruth Brown's savoir-faire. C'est
ça. Yeah they're her acolytes. She hires them to
chorus. Imagine, stage left Jake and Hank, humming
undertone and swaying with the beat. In the
lightbeam an empty mike. A drum-roll, the cue for
Cagey Jake who shouts *And now, time to get to the*

business. Let's hear it for (cue the horns) *the C.E.O. of soul, Ru-u-u-u-th Brown!* Out she struts into the light. And she's lookin', she's lookin' so-o-o-o good.

eyes, alight. in the mirror, as long as a photograph, smudges speak.

84.

Words you do not like insist. You hear them and
speak them. Would you be your friend among such
words if you were you? Were someone else? Clogged
by these words, you cough to clear your throat. Sun is
moving north. The angle of light bleaches words on
the screen. Everything white—such cleanliness is loss.
Just as well. The hurt and the hurting are past. You are
contained, though now fear dullness, your lines going
flat. So you ear-tune for music. Eye books for guidance
on poetry, on raising a child, the expression of love.
Not valentine glyphs but strong and tender words, soft
but resolute. How to be, how to extend your repertoire
to unlearn your narrow capacity, to learn the hard way
psalms of the future. spasm songs. words fall apart. branches of
the worth of *no*, or silence, that the void has value and
occupies space, to learn to guide your small wars
toward benefit. Outside, in newsspace words bomb
Saddam, his phono-ironic name, and dicker the
presidency of a man sucked by power and pain and
folly. You learn, but grow apprehensive at your
selective deafness, sluggish mouth, at a cluster of
syllables that stumble your tongue. You try to improve
its athleticism, tongue-crunching, ten at a time, twice
a day, and talking faster. You rap and wriggle your
tongue to tune its flabby capacity, and talk about talk,
forgetting to pause, practise tiny utterance, succulent
words. You forget the possibility of wordlessness,
believe that speech begins in the mouth. Not only in
the mouth.

86.

What is not seen is the only important thing. What
you see is evidence of the *not seen.* Threadweave, fibre-
word leads, holds together, pushes on. Ghost-wind. No
ruffles, but constant buffeting. Barely aware of it. Yes,
something propels, yet holds. You have symptoms—
thickness in the throat, stiff knuckles, needle-pain at
the heels, an ache behind eyes. Sight is trumped by this
malaise. You feel like an easy target and peer at the
calendar thinking this is progress though dates bleed
into each other and confuse. Ease is swiped from you
from all sides. Squinting left, right, or ahead, blur-
blind, barely aware of the filaments unbreezed but
grazing you. Now-veins run beneath. A kiss is too
your verve, your narrow capacity. your cluster-worn artifice. erasure
much for your cluster-worn artifice. Erasure and the
virus pales you, you succumb, drop out of the game,
drop to your bed vanishing to vanish to yourself. But
the aching head reminds you of yourself despite
delirium. You have accepted unreason, injustice,
emptiness, without lustre, without lust. Veil-eyed,
listless on the threadbare spike-bed. Yet hunger
compels you to rise for a meal, tumble liquid through
your cells. Perhaps the ailments will exit your pores
with bits of you attached. Perhaps here can be found
hope when your senses respond to the undercurrent's
trace. Stranded, you'll weave, upright at least, in the
needling air.

Dip cautiously in the *pleasure-holes of wordplay
that leak meaning.* Wordsplay. Killer-edged swordplay
of the tongue. Sure-holds and slippages that pay off,
pay more than lip service to the lip-licking muscle.
Lip-clicking word-drifts cast about for enticement,
sleek entry. Candle-aided. Wick lit or is it licked,
fingered, smouldering. Wordsmoke leaks toward the
vent. Invents slogans bent on converting you. Puts the
cons on, divests you. Of your comprehension, your
lexical fortune. Riches slip away through pocket-holes.
Flipped through some niched clique of sleight-
tonguers, who, sneer-lipped, live off avails. Off
available naifs who think they've taken the hundred-
includes you, leaves you haggard. wordsmoke leaking toward the vent,
proof sip, sealed the gist-holes, made them leak-proof.
They're hosed by soulless spoofers, cunning and
dunning gangsters, aloof as they fleece you, saying
pay-more-as-you-play. Catch my riff?

All things are less than they are, all are more. Like separation. Like fantasy lust clutched in a car on a backroad, winter closing in, locked door. I look for heat in the clench of delirium. Like the notion of politics as a train-coach, or an unhooked garment. I step in or out of an image at will, led by creeds believed to be radical, mildly at least. I thin, elongate, skinny as a shadow cast from low light, and straddle disarrangement, stretch between firmness and flux in my quest for serenity. (Beware the dead who walk and talk, shadowless.) I limit my quickening. I am not getting out enough. Everything I write comes from inside, not out in the real story. (Maybe I'm fibbing.)

skinny as a shadow cast from low light, clouded by drama, strange,

What do you think? Aches in my body replace ideas with dull lamentations that insist. My elbow burns against the arm-rest. I toe-test the possibility of disarray. A coward, were the truth told. (Told here?) I must rise to something beyond myself, beyond familiarity. I live not the wild way. Responsibilities create a quandary. I am not alone. There are those who are close, but I am multiple. How to lose the extras? I hear clicks, purchase a ticket, wait for appearance of the train's smoky stack (I'm in a movie), for the huge steel wheels to screech to a halt. My ticket is dateless, without a berth. Where to lie? I'll step back through the shades, writhe the sofa-wide sedan, steam the windows. I'll hide there in a shell.

Shapes from the grey outside come now. I'm lost in a
recall. A whiff of perfume. Her beauty in a posture of
willingness. Of more. Or less. In the heat I'd give up
everything I know. (Would I?) Wheels squeal and
sparks fly at the bend. I tilt in a steam-dizzy husk,
everything leans. Ready to fly off the track.

akimbo, undone. gambado and plié. suffering with weakness and

Hungry for words, I read: *to describe something already there, is to de-scribe, un-write.* To dis/cover into un-familiarity. Ur-zone. Murmurs last night at the reading. Words rattled and wrenched, clattered the air, fell to battened ears bracketing blank perplexity. I coughed, carried on. Got through, then drove into the dark, jolting coffee, peering for deer. Wind pushed me. I tuned in the radio to get lost in someone else's words. On static-crackles out of the night came *antibiotics, livestock.* Came *sustainable, super-bug, food for the world.* A sponge, I suck up these words the way night sucks light. I breathe, drink, watch, eat words— omnivorous, no weight or density is too great. I hoard **congestion, rules and the scaffold. back-pull out of your shell to the** and by day jab a few back to the air (tiny verse-probes). Everywhere else research digs and speaks to help humankind, pens goodsounding words to put me at ease. *Raloxifene, Elavil, Benylin.* I'll feel better soon, go on to more meaningful work. I'll drive a taxi through the ghazal-lit streets, nurse in wards filled with crisis and elegy. But here I poke around with juxta-position, hidden puns, cryptic reference. Messing with the *dis*, the *un*, and the dark. I don't know where I am. I'm de-worlded, written over, as relevant now as an Elvis-impersonator-in-a-white-jump-suit sighted in a tunnel in Moose Jaw. I'm a desperado, at work against hope. A dewlap on the throat of speech, I flap, crave, persist. I un-write. In the *un* is where to begin. I beg *un.*

93.

Wind is a biter. Black trees shelter me. It's a short walk to town but takes effort today due to indecision. Tongue is zinc-bitter, cheeks buffed apple-red. I take appropriate pills and liquids but the rheum lingers. I am at retreat from the pressures—a respite earned— where words are to flow like a Rocky Mountain stream in spring, like liturgy from the mouth of a priest. But I am choked off with fever and chill, with tight-chested hack. And the black, skeletal trees, aside from wind-break, offer no respite. Out there beyond Wolverine Creek the world carries on. I return to my tiny den. In Saskatoon no one cares that my desk is empty of imagination. In Sacramento no one knows that I am

void that is full. in the cells, cavities of necessary duty, life's random

in a small room suffering with weakness and congestion. In Valparaiso where Gerry writes and laughs between the Sierra de Los Filabres and the Mediterranean, no one knows that I am pressed down in a low-visibility front, under the weight of words I do not write, under the weariness of low-grade mid-winter melancholy. Even the temporary early evening rescue of Wintermint tea and chuckling, or the late cigary air with friends, Jamieson's and Cheezies, brings no cure. Now in the clotted quiet of a building that sleeps, no one, despite eccentricities, is up offering curatives. I grow desperate. Something wild and out-of-body might cure my malaise. Danger and intrigue in the dark night might spark verve in my muscles. I rasp, phlegmy, but dry of ideas. I rush into the night toward the black trees, calling. Draw faces to windows. Ahead, whispers slither through spruce-limbs to avoid me, twist away at the sound of this cough. How I run! How far must I chase to churn out of myself?

musical shuffle. yanked from your particular gravel and grass. wrench

Report from the front of the soon-to-form thoughts. *Get rid of all those bits of paper, whole, torn, folded, or not. It is man's body that is poetry, and the streets.* Traffic of phonemic breakdown, tongue-trilled, gurgling fricatives. "It is woman's body," I say. Flow, music, disjunction, polyvalence! Emotion and Thought and Form step through the arch, vamp the ramp in ill-fitted word-garb. I try to be pre-articulate. To catch that veil, that split-second flash at entrance. Grabbed in the shred between sensation and speech. *No longer speaking / Listening with the whole body.* Pulse that precedes breath ahead of *aaahh* on the entranced lips of the beholder. Far before the poise of
and adoration. magpie's shiny tail or a glistening grackle neck. feather-
syntax, the power-turn of co-option. How to break into that circuit, that pattern? I am reading, before shape, the architecture of lack. The back-pull to the void that is full but belies utterance. *tt tt tt ll ll aaahh.* A transient ischemic attack that jumbles my syllables, shakes the brain-bag and strains for utterance that stays locked behind clotted receptors. No one is safe. Not the customer, the costumer (I). I grope back for familiar, to propel *I* on. Am tempted to take it easy, to take the ramp, tramp the authorship trail, draw the lights to myself, not to the ions of speech. But I am un-authorized. Dispossessed. A faux phonologist, no matter what I say. *Who's the creator here anyway? Maybe language after all, despite itself.* I try, though it feels impossible, to reinvent my lips.

I stand in displacement with many tools to hook
me in, but sway, bewildered. My left foot moves
forward. My eyes gaze right through the walking
space. I am hooked to the globe, but am yanked from
my particular gravel and grass. I have not learned to
love hereness. Trees are on fire. Water is rising. I love
machines, their sur-human power. Yes my feet are here
in this flat place, among feathers, by the factory wall,
where the ground breaks. I am a schism, a schist, a
schistophrenic, and require medication, mediation,
meditation, divorced as I am. *Okay*, I say *Yank me!*
Yank me! Think I'm a doodle-dandy, just sucking
digital candy. Think I'm a bard and a barterer,
quiver, seasoned grin. a weed in the grass. a kernel, a seed that keeps
oblivious to the barb-bite. Sun is brightening. I'm
feeling better now, but for the vague sting in a part of
my flesh that's going numb. I can dull things by
ogling, collecting. Let's gather, let's tantra, let's
labyrinth. Repeat *Pentium, Coca-Cola, Hyundai, Dow.*
Pentium, Coca-Cola, Hyundai, Dow. Travel ads say I
can go anywhere anytime. So good to get away. I'm off.
But what is this jab, this jerk that jars my skull? No
matter. I can doff my head, flip it to the hook, wiggle
my toes. My feet may stumble, but my chicken-trunk
dances on.

97.

Numbers and names you could not dream back
then. So many beads fingered and beats of the heart.
Bread broken, crumbs that fall away. Blood cycles.
Uncountable. You have come through to this fraction.
This silver quarter of a century. Feather-quiver. I have
been reading about love, the many thousand words to
explain its languages. Words can make sense in the
right hands and ears. Does love? You fall, you touch,
you ignite, you clash and struggle. And one day you
are here. You behold. A testament to tenacity. You
pause at this way-station. Looking-place. Hawk-perch.
You see back. And ahead. You hear words. Of Cree, of
haematology. And sounds of desire and the gurgles of
on selling, combats people. by-pass and dispossess. by full methods
newborns. (*I meant to say other words, but as with desire
have veered, tongue-tripped.*) On your path, you have
touched many people. You have treated and healed.
Have spoken, given name and aspect to your story.
Friends pulse and feast with you, crest, crown, thermal
up with you, and today step close to share your
soaring-ground.

98. for Sky Dancer Louise and Peter B.

Yule pavilion. You'll go there. The way paved
annually. Lion paws prod your giftlist. You have loved
ones to signify, backspasms. Inamorato-wrought,
you're an artist of erotheism in stuff-orgied aisles filled
with the brand-witch rote spell, the isobaric theatre of
Yule fat. Of by-pass and dispossess. Abacus
representative, the retailer's frontispiece. The
frontward thrust of plastic. Contra-diction. In the
circus of confidence. Pain drops you to your knees.
You crumble. No horseback dancer, you. No tamer.
Your Interac card no help in this crumplage. Wince-
forced-pause. Slow-to-rise with searing. You pull
yourself together, albeit infirm. Art is collation.
of persuasion absconding with tranquility, embouchure. the music
Collagenation (social fracture anguish antidote). In-
jury. In-jection, in-timation. In-stability. In season. In-
scape. Inc.'s-rape. In-escapable as Santa, Manger-babe,
Bing Crosby. Yule fest of crepes and capons.
Spasmodic, pinch-nerved, inc.apacitated, you'll *learn
to think with pain.* You'll testify. Each birth, however,
holy.

Jimi sings *Foxy Lady*, ogles, tantras. Hand-trick-
slings his graceswung axe through mercury air. Picks
and slides, all motion, plucks steel strings with fingers,
teeth, and tongue. Everything liquifies, floats your
attention. Anthemic. In the wail you posit yourself.
Potential, anaemic, emphatic in a fortune-garden.
Torn between frailty, rage, and a wish, along with Jimi,
you set fire to the instrument, hope for music of
flame, mauve-singed fields of fireweed, the end of
something, chronology. "It's just rhythm," says
Prometheus, says Mallarmé. Listen to all tongues, their
rhythm speaking. Words empty themselves but he
keeps singing, *tired a wastin all my precious time.*
of flame. with frightful speed and swerves. skirmish in alphabets, in
Exhausted with twentieth-century disease, everything
pulses time-now, time-before. You will sacrifice, with
reluctance, to maintain today's privilege. Alarms
spasm in the deafening disintegration, dislocation of
millions. East of Eden are Kosovo, the Timor-row,
Afghani-scam, Iraq-attack-tak. *Make me wanna get up
and scream.* Jimi burned in his veins. Outfoxed, shot
through the loop hole of experience. Burned himself
up. Thirty-some years since. Arteries clog. Oxygen
tubes beckon. *Lady* is a bad word. Swift fox gnaws its
clenched leg. You stiffen, come to the raw, the marrow,
wailing. Jimi's ash-riffs still smoulder. Ember-bone.
Comin t'gitcha.

In knife-blade, in the sciss'd gap, the known
quakes, an instant cramps. Other cuts in.
Kolarborations. S(v)i(o)lence, a night hood, Jiri-rig on
syntax, etymology or derivation. Im-perspective
deviation from the eyes' shrouded logic. A window
opens without sound. (Terror-cue.) Unblinded. Pear
and apple in full view, covered with words that jostle,
that ache for a mouth to come before the skinning.
Fruits skittish and laden. My muslin-sack of words
falls to the floor with a thunk. *Who'd have thunk it?* she
used to say. I keep forgetting so emptiness looms but I
don't stop moving my lips. Cramp of loss stabs after
the quake. Spilled words scramble for order to
the quarries. ache for a mouth, sugared or sullied or serving. fa-la-la. to
camouflage me, and I appear as a pillar of virtue,
green-hued, leafy with syllables, accordioned with her
shape by a blade's application. Interleaved in this
instant, all that was. Snaky hissstory. The apple has
eyeseeds. The pear hears. That first tree is sheared,
naked, aching in the cataracting sky.

101.

Sometimes my book is sore is the way I mis-read
it. Had it massaged, stretched, drugged, soaked, rolled
on tennis balls. I bought a moulded seat and brace for
support, but the spine and tissue and glue still cramp
and crackle. Book, a spasm of words, a corner-point
jab. Book, a tile or brick, of before. A rear view mirror.
Mere roar of yore. Aching from a twist or splay, but
might sort the view by reverse or misread. Objects
may appear smaller or further away, cause me to
swerve. Book is a history of fractures. Gifted hands
might ease the misbinding. A vowel shifts, grows a
tail, has a chunk bitten off—b*oo*k is b*ac*k. To its old
self. Negative. Backwards, backwoods, backpedal,
come before the skinning, though you hear a distant whispering.
backhand, flashback, backflap. I don't know it's there
'til loss shows up. My own weight drops me to the
floor, to a wormy perspective. I want up, the uplifting
I expect from a book, sore or not. I'll read in recovery.
Letters unblurred in the mirror: *my book is* a stare; a
startle; *sometimes my book is* sorry, *is* a sword; *is*
sordid, and when finished its deed, skulks wordlessly
down a back stair in dim light. I can't tell, though I
try, my sore tale. I am the history of the future. Soft
tissue frays with age, its memory of youth, of first
editions. Spasms in a place the mirror can't see
cripple me and all because my eyes are going. Or is it
my brain? Definition fades. While I can, I'll re-open
the book. Search the line's real meaning. Book
another treatment, a book realignment.

102. after reading Robert Kroetsch's "Hornbook #[blank]"
in *The Hornbooks of Rita K.*

Stream current, circular. I keep at its swirls.
Paddling, drinking Ovaltine. Dizzied with repeat-
whirl. Revolving-gurge-tack-grasp for revelation. I'm
off. Tm-tm tm-tm tm-tm-tmm, you, Neil, sway, as
your bass-engine pulls up the trio's anchor. You
swing. You're a trough and crest shifter, sliding here
and there, fast, then slow, whatever the current needs.
Water pushes, pulls a sway-back ride. A back-bender,
you hunch over your craft, nimble ddl-ddl-ddl-ddl-
ddl-fingers dribbling down the gut strings. Your chart
sails over the tishing cymbal, and the wsh-wsh-skin-
brush. I reach for music with no instrument. I chop-
stroke using hands and feet, paddle-less, just re-ache
the day of bad news, the unendurable day, that blew the doors open.
the sprain. My ear fills with water, but I hear voices, a
refrain. Blink and I've missed the note. The future
slips behind me, then returns. Your bass-lines ripple
my radio and your big string-jazz-axe rumbles my
living room. At the window, whoosh-birds flicker,
ignite the air. Cat! Startle at the rail. Birds vanish,
one wingflick from a meal. Gleam in cat's eye shifts
to a squint of catty resignation, a so-what leap-down.
Coast is clear. Blue jay, note-cued drops to the rail
and juncos and sparrows and chickadees flit in the bush.
Brittle leaves rattle with fine-boned wing-boats. I can
feel your bass-thrum, Neil, in my chest, Weiling away
time in signatures, Monking around, savoury, sweet.
Wind taps the birdfeeder on my pane, a steady, jagged

beat. Where am *I*? Jazz-matazzed even as
diminuendo's tones hawk-hover my radio. I imagine
you slipping the big cover over the bass before you
shove off. Though you're hundreds of miles away, you
were here in my living room, in the boat with me, the
birds and that cat, floating on notes and words. We
were revving, tm-tm-heart-bass-rivering. Reverie
riffing my hull.

hammered through your pores. the deadly exchange in the curves of

103. for Neil Swainson

Some after words for John V. Hicks

You are taken. How slight my efforts seem now.
A few letters and calls. A visit here and there. And
intention. Your death was not convenient. My
appointment book was full. You had poems in mind.
Your ledger held blank pages. You'd stacked
symphonies to hear again. I had the future. Neglect
and omission are feeble bolts, soon anguish-sheared.
Your kitchen table was a weave of books, recordings,
mail, and pizza coupons. Poetry everywhere, visible
and not, charged the molecules of your living room
where we talked and laughed, full of cookies, tea, and
words. Screens fill but no script escapes absence. The
drying leaf, nibbled by air, crumbles beneath the
words. *the uplifting you expect from a book. can feel their words*
hedge of conifers. And now the *silence.* Silence you,
attuned, had overheard with your acute listening.
You caught the unhearable signal, that note at the
point of its breaking.   How I hedge. Cup over my
good ear. You chimed. Each peal, a resonant note,
and diminuendo. We are all a braid of sounding and
diminishment. Death, I suspect, is just so, and
without anxiousness. Death rings a secret, which
when revealed, unravels with its bearer. You now are
word-shorn, yet your words gather, they root and
branch, verse upon verse at my reach. But around
me a patter of noise and clench rattles my solemnity,
my intent. Yesterday I wondered where I was. Where
here? Earth in a galaxy in a universe of swirling

chunks and gases. There could be nothing at all.
What is a universe but patterns of our faces, hands,
in this room? I press ahead with your lines and mine,
with my ear uncovered, listening hard for your voice
and its after tones. There! Ash-rustle. *Whisper of a
single note descending.* Makes my craving ear ache,
makes it sing.

in your mouth though you cannot tongue them, tongue dusted

White fog breaks on the windshield. The road
appears and vanishes. We steer. Deer hover out there,
we are sure, at edges. We nibble our way. Most things
hide from the eye. Most of your body is invisible, but
science put you inside a peeking machine. You
couldn't move. Later you said it was noisy, a red-light
line above your nose and down the length of your
body. We try the high beams but these bring ghosts
alive on the screen. We switch back to low, turn on
defrost. We are hunched and winding toward your
house, squinting for signs. You are required to unhook
your rings, pendant, and metal utilities before
magnetic resonance magnifies your brain, slice by

thick, tallowy. vanishing into the dark. upturned faces wait. one hand

slice, while leaving you intact. You are stoic, static,
pretending a coffin. We pass Fulda (making guy-
jokes), Pilger, and Middle Lake, talk about love, its
primitive inexplicables. Words always a syllable-shift
short. Boxed in. We are pressed by fog, fear-rind. We
drop to the valley, the curtain peels back. We drive
past your house, made strange by new clarity. We turn
around. We sit to your table. Discuss the difference
between *connaître* and *savoir*. Clarify knowing amidst
the unknown, the implications of disease. The meal—
salad, chicken, rice, yellow beans—is simple and
lovely. Your dining room a treasure-box, exquisite. Fog
is forgotten. We talk of organs, flutes, Messaien and
multiple sclerosis, of computers and monks. The

bishop's red gloves are elegant on your hands. The wine has a melony nose. We rip the frill from the table cloth, hold the loop overhead. White circles us, turns about us. Turns us. Something about purification and unity. There is love here, perhaps even desire our syllables have not diagnosed. We are witty. You are relieved by technology. We talk of disposal of our bodies at the end of our time. We step outside to admire the glittering icicle-lights, their festive exuberance. The wind is cold. We contemplate the journey home, the necessity of re-entering the fog.

on the wheel, hand running up the inside, and a wrench. thrum

105. for Simon, Renée, and David

You pinball an intersection on slick ice. It's a
question of slippery advantage. Of capitalization.
According to the daily news you're not pursuing
money fast enough nor in the right places. Get
bonds, or bondage will lash you to the eternal
treadmill. You tire and your tires are too worn. So
much worry. So you hurry every day to set gain and
loss in the right columns. Speed to impending
deadlines, looming overdrafts, lean meals. Where is
elegance? You spin when it's time to move ahead,
jostle when you wish for calm. You are asleep when
you want to impress. Now you've found freedom in
ice-sliding. Like the friend who, skidding and
unheard. drying leaf, nibbled by air, crumbles. inside each of us
spinning down a highway, gave up, and when it
ended, she opened her eyes expecting eternity, but
found ditch-grass bobbing at her hood. No red-
riding. Just some feral grace that slipped her
through. Such wealth and without a broker (or was
it the one beyond naming). Clockhands scrape your
skin with every advance. The wolf stalks, is the
threatened one. Casino-trap is sprung. Bond tables
turn to grime on your fingers. At craps, indecision
possesses you. You are a fool, not understanding the
game. Blind to a market index, you have no
resources for stockplay. You take stock of what you
can. Decide on quality; attempt to become a better
lover. Not just technique, but in regard and
response. You will see how it goes, despite your

phobias. That clank again. Jeopardy. The sound of the crashing stockade. Will the new-fashioned *You* set you free? Will it confuse your lover? Or those who know you? You lift your foot off the gas and the brake. The car ricochets, clunks to a halt at the junction. The door pops, you leap out, the foothold so dicey you grab for the sky, the rouletting clouds.

a child wails at a fence. we talk of disposal of our bodies at the end of

106.

February. Month of saints and chivalry, heart-
takers, bowers and quiverers. And the quizzical Dada
inventor incanting onstage. Month of tenderness and
shivery cold. Depends where you live, on your altitude.
In chill some fall into age-gloom, the parchment
crimp of death. It is the month of *under the bridges of
Paris,* in Dada Zurich back eighty-six years. Of
Cabaret Voltaire where Hugo Ball, the magic bishop of
clouds and elephants, appeared with a be-attitude of
reverent irreverence. Month of crossbills and cupids at
your feeder. Of thinking through lips. Murmur of
romance swells offshore. An el niño of fetish drafts
eastward from the sea to market love. And Ball rolls on
our time. through the swoop of the day. dehiscent. truth a fugitive,
onstage, chants himself into glossolalia, into terror, 'til
he's carried off in his cylinder in a self-ordained sweat,
babbling of cats and peacocks, sea horses and flying
fish, the Lamb of God. From Dada to Deus with no
thought of chocolates and greeting cards. Heart-red
crest on the crowns of redpolls beaking your seeds.
Finches flash flame-orange. Month of welcomed
colour. It is no month to die. Frozen ground welcomes
no one. A strawbale set fire meets frosty resistance,
eventually tenders the soil. A hole can be scraped, but
who wants to rest there, given a choice. Ball bolts in a
flight out of time. A soaring fish, he isn't built for airy
distances, but reaches Swiss peaks in the spring
nonetheless. His beloved Emmy picks meadow-

lush wildflowers as birds magic-carpet the skies.
She sets poppies and edelweiss in a vase in the
shadowy room where he intones. She opens the
shutters to scurrying spiders and moths, the spilling
vermilion music of the sun. They turn to the light,
sing *blaulala loooo, hallelujah,* inventing the sounds
in their mouths.

a bright red scar, rust. clockhands scrape your skin. vicious circles

107.

In the winter morning dark I've just dashed you,
my son, to school. Now the sky breaks, a slash of white
vapour writes across the greyblue sky and that white
cord is your umbilicus, is your swaddling cloth, is the
gap I stepped across, five years four months ago.
Before then you were pre-occupation, you were
absence of love, you were career and distraction, you
were poems and performances and self-discovery. You
took a half century to get my attention with insistence
that hovered so long in the shadowy wings. I carried
you to my every stage, in my inattentions. You ghosted
my every word, my unknowing, until out of dimness a
turbulent light arced, caught something of a shape

scab. with conscientious use, the card of the hour. such is expected,
shown first in the drenched eyes of your mother-in-
waiting, another white ribbon yanked from the sky,
bowed and fixed to a gift that came in a torrent, a
storm-furl. She and I were current-churned,
unravelling. You were a wisp growing certain in the
diaphanous fold, awaiting. You waited in rivers, in
tousled beds, whispered in summer grasses and
snowdrifts. You were intention and chance, long
months of ideas. Then the opening, the unfurling. You
were a moment of heat, a convinced intuition, a list of
names, a shadow and heartbeat on a screen, a poking
limb. You were my pacing, her groaning, my counting,
3-4-5, nurses leaning, urging, her pushandpush. You
were resistance, your tiny self opposing debut in

the autumn gleam. You, despite your wish to be in our arms, determined to stay in that floating numberless world. You, a contrary patch of hair poking from the tunnel of your mother's flesh. 9-10-11-12, you, when certain of our attention, crashed into dawn, careening us, shaping our ardour.

unexpected. the frozen ground welcomes no one. loss is a constant. a

108. for Emmett and Jill

A letter wears down. Letters as wares weary you.
You are exhausted by poetry, an overhearing that
pushes you to bed. You read and overread, your *I*
moving across black grit. You are worn by pronominal
duality, pretense giving distance. *You*—I try to give up
Siamese pretending but have become used to being
someone else. Decide to accept *IYou* for a while.
Wounded ones cling. *MYour* history of this. The ones
IYou like, who have gaps. The Gary, the Ray, the Sol,
the Val. They cannot err with such luminous names. It
is not their chinks that draw you, but lack of pretense.
MYour equivalence. Perhaps it is exhaustion at failure.
MYour inability to press the poem to other tonality. To
yellow egg sitting on a sill is the shape of eternity. you are on a rope,
whom speak? *MYour* ear once deft, deafed by droning.
Sense brakes down without a STOP sign. Dim sum of
too many words that don't add up. Adept
disappearance of raison d'être. At breakfast dates and
raisins eaten on Shreddies. Strands soaken to mush.
IYou want fibre. Backbone. *YouI* keep wolfing down
nutrients hoping to scour malignant false selves. *YouI*
would not malign anyone. Perhaps mathematics, an
alignment of numbers, can assist. Make a poem with
imaginary digits or formulae. Where do they begin?
End? *IYou* will stop for coffee. Frothy habit, boost to
keep *IYou* going. Going for what? Just as *YouWe* know,
all breaks down. The poem eludes *YouI*. Yes, there is no
poem. STOP, it screams at *YouI* as it falls apart.

But *IYou* race trying to catch. Catch up. It will not yield. Will not. Will will not make it. Words will not make it. Making will not make it. *IYou* will not make it. This silly. This lonely. This prevent. This stutter. *IYou IYou.*

bound in this moment and know no way of getting off. the pressured

Spring in a robinsong. Trees hinting green.
The return of heat and walking in shorts. Roar of
street sweepers. Car-tires pinging gravel and rust.
You watch for a flash in the sky. A man *wears a*
necktie, drives in a car, alone. Over there, a woman
in that one. Combustionsparks spew. His car bears an
emblem of wings. The woman sports a tiara of blue
eggs and is proud. You turn left and scabbed at the
lips. *The folds in the earth.* Great keening begins.
Cannot stop the drying. Once-upon-a-spring, snow
geese did land on Tofield's plush plains. Now from
the highlands grizzlies lope down, hungry for fish.
The man wears a necktie of fire. A brush scrubs the
surround. *what to believe in. current-churned, unravelling. words*
curb in this season of rubble. You love the
disappearance of dust. But it stays. A girl on a bike
rides the gutter and stumbles. Hot metal growls at her
bones in a flash. You are on the far walk and want to
reach out. Slowing you, your boots of fieldstone and
gloves of woven ash. *The folds in the earth overflow*
with tears. Drivers blinded by speed. Cars and
sweatshirts and towers bear an emblem of wings. The
tiara-graced woman is proud of thickening goo in her
hair. The tie-adorned man grabs at his neck too late;
his head is in flames. From the salt- and rust-chafed
folds of your skin a scream wails through the hole in
the sky. The flyway is wingless. Snow geese glide not
to Tofield's parched plains.

110.

r symbols

a path too difficult to hold

word

go swimming past in the unknowable current. shot upon arrival,

111. ghost-poem

to se
ttle, settle in the na
ked day. I, reft, be sec
tioned from the o
nes that matter. I be rou
gh on insides, my own, my in
terior sorrow growing with the ar
c of s
un across the sky. the down
ness of it. the way those lo
ved can hu
rt themselves, hurting me me hurting them. and the un
deserved suffering of an eld

wounded ones cling. terror, all hooks and twine. remote control. path
er one the one I love, hove to. torn to
day from. father wife son all tum
ble in me. hooks and twine and tug
ging. father knock
ed down ag
ain, the System (cyst-m) wins one more. lover in own dis
tress hurls eyebarbs & stern
words, steers aw
ay. son tests and tests for pow
er, then turns love loose turns me over. flip and wri
ggle like some fish (so easy to say 'out of water'.) but I dro
wn there. I am I, twi
sting, never mind the me

dium. liquid or g
as I do not wish this for you or tho
se you love. we watch bits and chunks of ourselves ta
ken day by day. we de(us)
serve much be
tter, debt to life set
tled long ago we de(us)serve m
ore reward than we clutch in hand to
day, bent in end
less s
tru
g
gle
too difficult. the appearance of a dark ligament. a stark bone, a

crumbling tongue fluttering in your palm. gloves of woven ash.

I write to speak to those I have heard.

—Louise Glück

Notes on sources, quotations and allusions.

Epigraph
"To think? . . . To think! It is to lose the thread."
Paul Valery, quoted in Maurice Blanchot, *The Writing of the Disaster*
(Lincoln: University of Nebraska Press,1986), 107.

"May words cease to be arms; means of action, means of salvation.
Let us count, rather, on disarray."
Maurice Blanchot, *The Writing of the Disaster*, 11.

Epigraph to Notes
"I write to speak to those I have heard."
Louise Glück, in *Proofs & Theories: Essays on Poetry* (Hopewell, NJ:
The Ecco Press, 1994), 128.

#5
th'read.
From bpNichol & Eleanor Nichol, *thread* (Toronto: Underwhich
Editions, 1987). Out of print.

#6
Aqueduct.
Gerry Shikatani, *Aqueduct: Poems and Texts from Europe, 1979–1987*
(Toronto: Mercury Press / Underwhich Editions / Wolsak & Wynn
Publishers, 1996).

#15
the prostitutes of etymology.
Blanchot's actual phrase is the "postulates of etymology," in *The
Writing of the Disaster*, 103.

#24
lunar knowledge . . . share.
Birthdates: Robert Kroetsch: June 26, 1927
            Steven Ross Smith: June 25, 1945

first the tide rushes in.
From "Ebb Tide," by The Platters, on Mercury Records, May 1960.
(Hum it if you can.)

listen for thunder on cloudless days.
Robert Kroetsch, correspondence with the author, 17 October 1996.

#25
It is raw, beckons ... otherwise.
Reference to, but not a quote: Milosz recalls Blanchot recalls
Wittgenstein.

The mathematics of the gaze: angle and tangent.
Robert Kroetsch, "Noosa Heads 2," in "Spending the Morning on the
Beach," in *Completed Field Notes* (Toronto: McClelland & Stewart,
1989), 257.

a pleased and luminous and violent desire.
Robert Kroetsch, "The Veil of Knowing," in *The Lovely Treachery of
Words* (Toronto: Oxford University Press,1989), 194.

It's a matter of knowing when to look and when not to look.
Robert Kroetsch, "Noosa Heads 2," in "Spending the Morning on the
Beach," in *Completed Field Notes,* 257.

#27
you're going to die of love.
Robert Kroetsch, Old Lady Lang to Liebhaber, in *What the Crow Said*
(Toronto: Paperjacks, 1978).

aporrhoea.
An emanation, effluvium.

the poem must resist the poet.
Robert Kroetsch, in "The Sad Phoenician," in *Completed Field Notes,*
61.

#30
such edges of the trembling soul.
Robert Kroetsch, "Letters to Salonika, June 25," in *Advice to My
Friends* (Don Mills: Stoddart Publishers,1985), 68.

the old / poet, in his cups / and thinking. Ibid.

he got the color of his breast / from the heat of the setting sun!
Charles Olson, "The Kingfishers," in *The Distances* (New York: Grove
Press, 1960), 6.

#31
References to Robert Kroetsch, *What the Crow Said.*

#32
In the death of your mother I speak to the grass.
Reference to Robert Kroetsch, "The Poet's Mother, 1," in *Advice to My
Friends,* 139.

she could name the ducks in the dark by their talking.
Reference to Robert Kroetsch, "Sonnet for My Daughters," in *Advice
to My Friends,* 136.

attention is the natural prayer of the soul.
"Celan cites Benjamin citing Mandelbranche in his essay on Kafka,"
as noted in "from Shibboleth," in Jacques Derrida, *Acts of Literature*
(New York: Routledge, 1992), 384. Original source, *Gesammelte
Werke in funf Banden,* ed. B. Alleman and S. Reichert (Frankfurt am
Main: Suhrkamp, 1983). Also quoted in J. Felstiner, *Paul Celan: Poet,
Survivor, Jew* (New Haven: Yale University Press, 1995).

words are pretenders.
Robert Kroetsch, "Sounding the Name," in *Advice to My Friends,* 134.

Niemand.
Reference to Paul Celan's "Psalm."

#34
rat-a-tat-Rita.
Reference to Robert Kroetsch, *The Hornbooks of Rita K* (Edmonton:
University of Alberta Press, 2001).

Dragland.
Stan Dragland.

Draper.
Gary Draper.

yakety-yak don't talk back
From "Yakety-Yak," The Coasters, Atco Records, April 1958.

All pieces in the "Suite for Robert Kroetsch" included here and in *fluttertongue book 2* were written for presentation at A Likely Story, a celebration of Robert Kroetsch—the man, his writing, and his 70th birthday, at St. Jerome's University, University of Waterloo, June 1997. The pieces appeared in earlier versions in *The New Quarterly* XVIII, 1 (1998).

#36.
bone-ladder.
Jean (Hans) Arp, "The Man, The Woman," in *Arp on Arp. Poems, Essays, Memories,* trans. Joachim Neugroschel (New York: The Viking Press, 1972), 179.

the lips of the tombs are alive,
Jean (Hans) Arp, "The Sky Is an Egg," in *Arp on Arp,* 174.

#50
Horse-songs of Frank Mitchell.
Composer-performer Jerome Rothenberg (variously performed, published, and recorded). For one example, see *Poems for the Millennium*, vol. 1, ed. J. Rothenberg and P. Joris (Berkeley: University of California Press, 1995), 767.

#52
Jill.
J. Jill Robinson, fiction writer, spouse of S.R. Smith.

#58
You too Nicky.
Reference to bpNichol, *Gifts: The Martyrology Book[s] 7&* (Toronto: Coach House Press,1990). Unpaginated. (Near the end.)

#65
what the eye seizes as real is fractured again and again.
bpNichol, "Scraptures: 17th Sequence," in *Gifts: The Martyrology Book[s] 7&.*

saying, I said you should be writing things down.
bpNichol, "The Book of Days, 1966–1971," in *Craft Dinner* (Toronto: Aya Press, 1978), 3.

the frontiers of madness.
Clarice Lispector, *Selected Crônicas,* trans. Giovanni Pontiero (New York: New Directions Publishing,1992), 179.

the farmhouse door / bangs against the skull.
bpNichol, *monotones* "LXII" (Vancouver: Talonbooks, 1971). Unpaginated.

#67
Written while reading bpNichol," hour 24: 11:35 a.m. to 12:35 p.m.," in *Martyrology Book 6* (Toronto: Coach House Press, 1987). Unpaginated. See particularly:

> *our songs fleeting, temporal,*
> *against these larger musics*
> *we glimpse notation of*
> *but never hear*

#71
and I shall be renewed by salt, ... I'll taste the dreams ... blown with the dust.
Aleksei Kruchenykh, "From the Sahara to America," in *Poems for the Millennium,* vol. 1, 237.

#74
if you wait out the dream the waking comes, and *Of the last wings.*
Source lost, though might have been an overhearing, or perhaps the author quoting himself.

#79
grow more heavy, be more light.
Paul Celan,*What occurred?,* from "Die Niemandsrose" in *Poems of Paul Celan,* trans. Michael Hamburger (New York: Persea Books, 1995), 209.

#80
tiny eternities.
Paul Celan, "Les Globes," from "Die Niemandsrose" in *Poems of Paul Celan,* 215.

#86
dicker the presidency of a man sucked by power.
USA, 1998, again and again.

#87
what is not seen is the only important thing.
Maurice Blanchot, "The Ease of Dying," in *The Blanchot Reader*, ed.
Michael Holland, trans. Michael Syrotinski (Oxford: Blackwell
Publishing, 1996), 301.

#91
pleasure-holes of wordplay that leak meaning.
Daphne Marlatt, *Readings from the Labyrinth* (Edmonton: NeWest
Publishers, 1998), 117.

#92
all things are less than they are, all are more.
Paul Celan, "Cello entry," from "Atemwende" *Poems of Paul Celan*,
261.

#93
to describe something already there, is to de-scribe, un-write.
Daphne Marlatt, *Readings from the Labyrinth*, 140.

#96
Get rid of all those bits of paper, whole, torn, folded or not. It is man's
body that is poetry, and the streets.
Henri Chopin, from *Poésie Sonore*, quoted in *Poems for the*
Millennium, vol. 2, 427.

No longer speaking / Listening with the whole body.
Muriel Rukeyser, "The Speed of Darkness," in *Poems for the*
Millennium, vol. 2, 70.

Who's the creator here anyway? Maybe language after all, despite itself.
Daphne Marlatt, *Readings from the Labyrinth*, 126.

#99
learn to think with pain.
Maurice Blanchot, *The Writing of the Disaster*, 145.

#100
Dedicated to Jimi Hendrix, my R'n'R & R'n'B & psychedelic hero. *I'm tired a wastin all my precious time; make me wanna get up and scream; comin t'gitcha.*
From *Foxy Lady* by Jimi Hendrix, first performed, it seems, in Honolulu, 5 October 1968. Here's to you, Jimi, wherever you are.

#101
kolarborations . . . jiri-rig.
Reference to Jiri Kolar, Czechoslovakian poet and visual poet (1914–2002).

unblinded.
Reference to Steven Ross Smith, "Vessel," in *fluttertongue, book 1: The Book of Games,* 66.

pear and apple in full view.
Reference to *Pear,* 1969, and *An Apple for Mr. K.,* 1972, visual works by Jiri Kolar.

#102
The Oviedo Hornbooks. Robert Kroetsch & Cuardernos de Literatura Postcolonial (Oviedo, Spain: Universidad de Oviedo,1999), 10–12.

104
silence.
In John V. Hicks, "And I give you the cry . . . the silence like ashes," in "Ascent to Silence," in *Silence Like the Sun* (Saskatoon: Thistledown Press, 1983), 73.

Whisper of a single note descending.
John V. Hicks, "Hours Secular, Matins and Lauds," in *Rootless Tree* (Saskatoon: Thistledown Press, 1985), 155.

#107
Hugo Ball.
Dadaist, organizer & performer at the Cabaret Voltaire, 1917, Zurich.

Emmy Hennings.
Dada artist/performer and wife of Ball.

flight out of time.
Title of Hugo Ball's journals (New York: The Viking Press, 1974).

vermilion music of the sun. Hugo Ball's, "The Sun," in *Poems for the Millennium,* vol. 1, 292.

blaulala loooo.
Part of a line from Hugo Ball's, "Gadji Beri Bimba," sound poem.

#108
Emmett.
Emmett H Robinson Smith, son of the author.

#110
The man wears a necktie of fire and *The folds in the earth overflow with tears.*
Jean (Hans) Arp, "The Man. The Woman," in *Arp on Arp,* 179.

~

The author gratefully acknowledges journal and electronic publications, which have published the following pieces:

24., 25., 27., 30., 31., 32., published in *The New Quarterly* XVIII, 1 (1998).

22., 36., 48., 50., published on the *East Village Poetry Web: Volume 4, The Poetries of Canada* (1998).

5., 15., 42., 58., 65., published in *Open Letter* 10, 4 (Fall 1998).

20., published in *filling station* 17 (1999).

22., 59., published in *Rampike* 11, 1 (May 2000).

1., 6., 15., published in *The Cafe Review* V, 11 (Spring 2000).

51., 93., published in *dANDelion* (June 2000).

108., published in *Contemporary Verse 2* 23, 4 (Spring 2001).

7., published in *Tart* eleven (Fall 2002).

97., 107., published in *Rampike* 13,1 (Winter 2002).

53., published in *Listening with the Ear of the Heart,* ed. D. Margoshes and S. Sopher (Muenster, SK: St. Peter's Press, 2003).

21., 86., published in *Qwerty* (Fall 2003).

21., 36., published in *A-Z Poems.* From V. Encontro Internacional de Poetas (Portugal: Faculdade de Letras da Universidade de Coimbra, 2004).

36., published in *LRC: Literary Review of Canada,* 12, 7 (September 2004).